About Skill Builders Math

by Carolyn Chapman

Welcome to RBP Books' Skill Builders series. Like our Summer Bridge Activities collection, the Skill Builders series is designed to make learning both fun and rewarding.

Skill Builders 4th Grade Math provides students with focused practice to help them reinforce and develop math skills. Each Skill Builders volume is grade-level appropriate, with clear examples and instructions. In accordance with NCTM standards, exercises for grade four cover a variety of math skills, including addition, subtraction, multiplication, division, word problems, geometry, graphing, time, money values, fractions, and decimals.

A critical thinking section includes exercises to help develop higher order thinking skills.

Learning is more effective when approached with an element of fun and enthusiasm—just as most children approach life. That's why the Skill Builders combine entertaining and academically sound exercises with eye-catching graphics and fun themes—to make reviewing basic skills fun and effective, for both you and your budding scholars.

W9-ATL-495

© 2003, 2004 RBP Books
All rights reserved
www.summerbridgeactivities.com

Table of Contents

Rounding Round-up

Round each number to the nearest ten.

1. 27 __**30**__   **2.** 57 _____   **3.** 78 _____

42 _____   33 _____   61 _____

39 _____   96 _____   47 _____

65 _____   11 _____   83 _____

Round each number to the nearest hundred.

4. 347 _____   **5.** 921 _____   **6.** 843 _____

626 _____   469 _____   277 _____

148 _____   515 _____   351 _____

511 _____   745 _____   678 _____

Round each number to the nearest thousand.

7. 7,649 _____   **8.** 3,129 _____   **9.** 2,199 _____

5,240 _____   8,490 _____   1,672 _____

3,971 _____   6,200 _____   4,721 _____

4,293 _____   1,221 _____   1,228 _____

© RBP Books   Math Grade 4—RBP0032

Rounding Round-up

1. What is 21,507 rounded to the nearest hundred?___**21,500**___

2. What is 8,987 rounded to the nearest thousand? _____

3. What is 214,299 rounded to the nearest thousand? _____

4. What is 718 rounded to the nearest ten? _____

5. What is 5,877 rounded to the nearest thousand? _____

6. What is 3,301 rounded to the nearest hundred?_____

7. What is 611,603 rounded to the nearest ten?_____

Round each number to the nearest ten.

8. At Viewmont Elementary, there are 59 students in the

fourth grade._____

9. In Mr. Randall's class, 23 students have a dog. _____

10. In Marc's school, 49 students play an instrument._____

Round each number to the nearest hundred.

11. Last year, 1,356 sandwiches were eaten in the cafeteria._____

12. The school library has 3,430 books. _____

13. Marcy's class used 239 crayons. _____

 © RBP Books

Lisa is studying populations in her geography class. Help her complete the chart below.

Place	Population	Rounded to Thousands	Rounded to Hundreds
Anchorage, Alaska	**260,283**	**260,000**	**260,300**
Sedona, Arizona	10,192		
Oceanside, California	161,029		
Boca Raton, Florida	74,764		
Burley, Idaho	9,316		
Sioux City, Iowa	85,013		
Baton Rouge, Louisiana	227,818		
Jackson, Missouri	11,947		
Missoula, Montana	57,053		
Las Vegas, Nevada	478,434		
Aztec, New Mexico	6,378		
Albany, New York	95,658		
El Paso, Texas	563,662		
Salt Lake City, Utah	181,743		

© RBP Books

Write the number for the words below.

1. nine thousand two hundred twenty-one _____ **9,221** _____

2. thirty-two thousand sixty-four _____

3. eight hundred forty-nine _____

4. seven hundred eighty-three thousand six hundred _____

_____

5. four hundred ninety-five _____

6. eight hundred eighty-eight thousand seven hundred twenty-five

_____

Write the words that describe the numbers below.

7. 2,943 _____

8. 10,811 _____

9. 7,246 _____

10. 112,161 _____

11. 1,641 _____

12. 90,012 _____

©RBP Books

How to write a check:

Write the name of the person or company you're paying here.

Write the dollar amount here.

Maria Smith
123 Anytown
Anywhere, UT

Date _____

Pay to the order of _____ $ _____

_____ Dollars

Spell out the dollar amount here.

Remember to sign your name on the check.

Maria is paying her monthly bills. Help her finish writing her checks.

1.

Maria Smith
123 Anytown
Anywhere, UT

Date _____

Pay to the order of **Toy Time** $ **14.00**

_____ Dollars

_____

2.

Maria Smith
123 Anytown
Anywhere, UT

Date _____

Pay to the order of **Electronic Station** $ _____

Five hundred thirty-three _____ Dollars

_____

3.

Maria Smith
123 Anytown
Anywhere, UT

Date _____

Pay to the order of **Furniture Barn** $ **784.00**

_____ Dollars

_____

© RBP Books

Write the number that means the same as:

1. 40,000 + 3,000 + 400 + 70 + 3

43,473

2. 50,000 + 5,000 + 600 + 20 + 7

3. 70,000 + 4,000 + 400 + 80 + 5

4. 450,000 + 8,000 + 100 + 40 + 7

5. 620,000 + 6,000 + 300 + 50 + 1

6. 780,000 + 70,000 + 500 + 20 + 8

7. 120,000 + 50,000 + 4,000 + 600 + 8

8. 900,000 + 300,000 + 10,000 + 400 + 20

6

Name the Number

Write the number that means the same as:

1. 5 hundreds, 9 tens, and 3 ones

_____

2. 14 thousands, 6 hundreds, 5 tens, and 0 ones

_____

3. 40 thousands, 7 hundreds, 3 tens, and 6 ones

_____

4. 1 hundred, 5 tens, and 4 ones

_____

5. 27 thousands, 3 hundreds, 8 tens, and 1 one

_____

6. 3 thousands, 4 hundreds, 6 tens, and 4 ones

_____

7. 91 thousands, 4 hundreds, 7 tens, and 5 ones

_____

8. 7 hundreds, 6 tens, and 3 ones

_____

© RBP Books

Work each problem.

1.

$$\begin{array}{r} \overset{1\,1}{2,176} \\ +\ 4,649 \\ \hline \mathbf{6,825} \end{array}$$

$$\begin{array}{r} 83,245 \\ +\ 76,487 \\ \hline \end{array}$$

$$\begin{array}{r} 61,209 \\ +\ 46,557 \\ \hline \end{array}$$

$$\begin{array}{r} 55,701 \\ +\ 31,976 \\ \hline \end{array}$$

2.

$$\begin{array}{r} 76,541 \\ +17,673 \\ \hline \end{array}$$

$$\begin{array}{r} 21,761 \\ +\ 83,174 \\ \hline \end{array}$$

$$\begin{array}{r} 56,405 \\ +\ 31,706 \\ \hline \end{array}$$

$$\begin{array}{r} 95,423 \\ +\ 5,760 \\ \hline \end{array}$$

3.

$$\begin{array}{r} 19,761 \\ +23,885 \\ \hline \end{array}$$

$$\begin{array}{r} 59,266 \\ +\ 30,195 \\ \hline \end{array}$$

$$\begin{array}{r} 76,511 \\ +\ 37,199 \\ \hline \end{array}$$

$$\begin{array}{r} 65,198 \\ +\ 11,279 \\ \hline \end{array}$$

4.

$$\begin{array}{r} 4,317 \\ 6,182 \\ +\ 9,502 \\ \hline \end{array}$$

$$\begin{array}{r} 6,111 \\ 7,963 \\ +\ 8,205 \\ \hline \end{array}$$

$$\begin{array}{r} 1,251 \\ 9,116 \\ +\ 7,197 \\ \hline \end{array}$$

$$\begin{array}{r} 9,761 \\ 4,317 \\ +\ 6,672 \\ \hline \end{array}$$

5.

$$\begin{array}{r} 1,257 \\ 6,491 \\ 7,644 \\ +\ 5,345 \\ \hline \end{array}$$

$$\begin{array}{r} 8,219 \\ 1,515 \\ 4,602 \\ +\ 5,617 \\ \hline \end{array}$$

$$\begin{array}{r} 4,117 \\ 7,649 \\ 3,444 \\ +\ 5,002 \\ \hline \end{array}$$

$$\begin{array}{r} 3,547 \\ 6,129 \\ 4,570 \\ +\ 2,001 \\ \hline \end{array}$$

www.summerbridgeactivities.com

©RBP Books

Work each problem.

1.

$$\begin{array}{r} \overset{1\,1}{1,166} \\ +\ 3,549 \\ \hline \mathbf{4,715} \end{array}$$

$$\begin{array}{r} 3,853 \\ +\ 6,485 \\ \hline \end{array}$$

$$\begin{array}{r} 8,432 \\ +\ 4,887 \\ \hline \end{array}$$

$$\begin{array}{r} 5,973 \\ +\ 3,689 \\ \hline \end{array}$$

2.

$$\begin{array}{r} 47,571 \\ +\ 37,773 \\ \hline \end{array}$$

$$\begin{array}{r} 94,752 \\ +\ 80,745 \\ \hline \end{array}$$

$$\begin{array}{r} 46,784 \\ +\ 38,134 \\ \hline \end{array}$$

$$\begin{array}{r} 67,470 \\ +\ 5,679 \\ \hline \end{array}$$

3.

$$\begin{array}{r} 13,341 \\ +\ 75,485 \\ \hline \end{array}$$

$$\begin{array}{r} 87,276 \\ +\ 45,555 \\ \hline \end{array}$$

$$\begin{array}{r} 65,971 \\ +\ 58,707 \\ \hline \end{array}$$

$$\begin{array}{r} 45,688 \\ +\ 11,659 \\ \hline \end{array}$$

4.

$$\begin{array}{r} 435,087 \\ +\ 51,587 \\ \hline \end{array}$$

$$\begin{array}{r} 843,245 \\ +\ 746,487 \\ \hline \end{array}$$

$$\begin{array}{r} 541,569 \\ +\ 786,598 \\ \hline \end{array}$$

$$\begin{array}{r} 689,778 \\ +\ 31,236 \\ \hline \end{array}$$

5.

$$\begin{array}{r} 7,256 \\ 6,686 \\ 4,674 \\ +\ 1,565 \\ \hline \end{array}$$

$$\begin{array}{r} 9,223 \\ 1,895 \\ 4,623 \\ +\ 7,874 \\ \hline \end{array}$$

$$\begin{array}{r} 6,457 \\ 7,875 \\ 3,669 \\ +\ 4,007 \\ \hline \end{array}$$

$$\begin{array}{r} 7,556 \\ 2,167 \\ 7,570 \\ +\ 1,005 \\ \hline \end{array}$$

© RBP Books

Put the correct sign (>, <, =) in each equation.

1. 9,743 $>$ 9,347

2. 16,021 $\bigcirc$ 16,201

3. 547 $\bigcirc$ 500

4. 123,972 $\bigcirc$ 123,792

5. 31,101 $\bigcirc$ 31,001

6. 607,916 $\bigcirc$ 607,916

7. 84,400 $\bigcirc$ 84,040

8. 4,729 $\bigcirc$ 4,927

9. 264,609 $\bigcirc$ 264,069

10. 509,621 $\bigcirc$ 509,621

11. 101,000 $\bigcirc$ 110,000

12. 11,001 $\bigcirc$ 11,101

13. 2,549 $\bigcirc$ 2,459

14. 679,401 $\bigcirc$ 679,041

www.summerbridgeactivities.com
©RBP Books

Write the correct sign in the problems below.

1. 2×4 $\bigcirc$ $2 \overline{)\, 4}$

2. $6 + 12$ $\bigcirc$ $6 \overline{)\, 12}$

3. $10 + 5$ $\bigcirc$ $5 + 10$

4. $9 \overline{)\, 72}$ $\bigcirc$ $8 \overline{)\, 64}$

5. 6×7 $\bigcirc$ 7×4

6. 8×4 $\bigcirc$ 3×12

7. $5 \overline{)\, 20}$ $\bigcirc$ $4 \overline{)\, 20}$

8. 4×7 $\bigcirc$ $9 \overline{)\, 72}$

9. $6 \overline{)\, 36}$ $\bigcirc$ $9 \overline{)\, 54}$

10. $4 \overline{)\, 16}$ $\bigcirc$ $3 \overline{)\, 12}$

11. 2×9 $\bigcirc$ $6 \overline{)\, 48}$

12. 4×5 $\bigcirc$ 3×6

© RBP Books

Solve each problem.

1.
$$\begin{array}{r} 8\,1 \\ 7\cancel{9}2 \\ -437 \\ \hline \textbf{355} \end{array}$$

$$\begin{array}{r} 641 \\ -482 \\ \hline \end{array}$$

$$\begin{array}{r} 249 \\ -196 \\ \hline \end{array}$$

$$\begin{array}{r} 571 \\ -198 \\ \hline \end{array}$$

2.
$$\begin{array}{r} 151 \\ -57 \\ \hline \end{array}$$

$$\begin{array}{r} 466 \\ -367 \\ \hline \end{array}$$

$$\begin{array}{r} 792 \\ -197 \\ \hline \end{array}$$

$$\begin{array}{r} 923 \\ -678 \\ \hline \end{array}$$

3.
$$\begin{array}{r} 954 \\ -199 \\ \hline \end{array}$$

$$\begin{array}{r} 671 \\ -297 \\ \hline \end{array}$$

$$\begin{array}{r} 897 \\ -692 \\ \hline \end{array}$$

$$\begin{array}{r} 634 \\ -459 \\ \hline \end{array}$$

4.
$$\begin{array}{r} 8,521 \\ -7,927 \\ \hline \end{array}$$

$$\begin{array}{r} 6,452 \\ -5,296 \\ \hline \end{array}$$

$$\begin{array}{r} 1,491 \\ -1,367 \\ \hline \end{array}$$

$$\begin{array}{r} 3,421 \\ -1,987 \\ \hline \end{array}$$

5.
$$\begin{array}{r} 9,621 \\ -2,999 \\ \hline \end{array}$$

$$\begin{array}{r} 4,492 \\ -3,198 \\ \hline \end{array}$$

$$\begin{array}{r} 6,115 \\ -5,977 \\ \hline \end{array}$$

$$\begin{array}{r} 1,271 \\ -1,186 \\ \hline \end{array}$$

RememBer... Include the comma in your answer!

©RBP Books

Solve each problem.

1.

$$\begin{array}{r} 674 \\ -\ 567 \\ \hline \end{array}$$
$$\begin{array}{r} 788 \\ -\ 299 \\ \hline \end{array}$$
$$\begin{array}{r} 459 \\ -\ 285 \\ \hline \end{array}$$
$$\begin{array}{r} 741 \\ -\ 478 \\ \hline \end{array}$$

2.

$$\begin{array}{r} 564 \\ -\ 87 \\ \hline \end{array}$$
$$\begin{array}{r} 857 \\ -\ 169 \\ \hline \end{array}$$
$$\begin{array}{r} 596 \\ -\ 478 \\ \hline \end{array}$$
$$\begin{array}{r} 848 \\ -\ 279 \\ \hline \end{array}$$

3.

$$\begin{array}{r} 323 \\ -\ 99 \\ \hline \end{array}$$
$$\begin{array}{r} 683 \\ -\ 176 \\ \hline \end{array}$$
$$\begin{array}{r} 654 \\ -\ 364 \\ \hline \end{array}$$
$$\begin{array}{r} 743 \\ -\ 455 \\ \hline \end{array}$$

4.

$$\begin{array}{r} 4,552 \\ -\ 2,327 \\ \hline \end{array}$$
$$\begin{array}{r} 5,442 \\ -\ 1,288 \\ \hline \end{array}$$
$$\begin{array}{r} 4,443 \\ -1,347 \\ \hline \end{array}$$
$$\begin{array}{r} 3,001 \\ -\ 1,867 \\ \hline \end{array}$$

5.

$$\begin{array}{r} 32,450 \\ -\ 5,869 \\ \hline \end{array}$$
$$\begin{array}{r} 54,532 \\ -\ 2,865 \\ \hline \end{array}$$
$$\begin{array}{r} 45,083 \\ -\ 4,907 \\ \hline \end{array}$$
$$\begin{array}{r} 51,533 \\ -\ 34,543 \\ \hline \end{array}$$

© RBP Books

Skates
$64.21

Shoes
$36.15

Socks
$5.68

Candy
$2.51

Pizza
$4.62

Baseball
Mitt
$19.33

www.summerbridgeactivities.com

©RBP Books

Mall Mania

Jason and his friends went to the mall. Use the information on the price tags to solve the problems.

1. Jason buys a slice of pizza. Then he buys a pair of socks. How much does Jason spend altogether?_____

_____

2. Mason buys a baseball mitt. If he gives the sales clerk a $20.00 bill, how much money does he get back? _____

_____

3. Eliza buys three pair of socks. How much does she spend altogether?_____

4. Rex has $50.00 in his wallet. He buys a pair of shoes. Does he have enough money left to buy a baseball mitt?_____

_____

5. Meg buys candy, a baseball mitt, and a slice of pizza. How much does she spend altogether? _____

6. At the mall, Tony buys a pair of skates and pays full price. His sister buys a pair of skates on sale for $59.65. How much more money did Tony spend than his sister? _____

_____

©RBP Books
Math Grade 4—RBP0032

Mr. Roberts is figuring class grades based on the number of points each student has earned. Estimate each student's total number of points.

1. Peter: 46, 88, 74 _____ $50 + 90 + 70 = 210$

2. Lucy: 69, 87, 91 _____

3. Abby: 55, 98, 44 _____

4. Morgan: 99, 97, 93 _____

5. Jake: 41, 56, 76 _____

6. Beth: 86, 88, 78 _____

7. Anne: 66, 72, 81 _____

8. Molly: 47, 58, 94 _____

©RBP Books

Candy Costs

Estimate the cost of each person's candy purchase.

Price List	
Licorice . . . . .13¢	Candy bar . . . . . . .87¢
Gumdrops . . . . . . .07¢	Gumballs . . . . .34¢
Package of gummy bears . . . . 56¢	

1. Jason buys 2 pieces of licorice and a package of gummy

bears. _____

2. Alexis buys a candy bar and 2 gumballs. _____

3. Mike buys 4 gumballs and a piece of licorice._____

4. Susan buys 3 packages of gummy bears._____

5. Ramona buys 1 candy bar, 2 gumballs, and a piece of licorice.

_____

6. Eric buys a piece of licorice, 10 gumdrops, and 1 gumball.

_____

7. Ryan buys 3 gumballs, 4 gumdrops, and 5 pieces of licorice.

_____

8. Jan buys 4 candy bars and 2 packages of gummy bears.

_____

© RBP Books

Point the Way

Plot the points on the coordinate system below.

1. (4,0)

2. (-3,4)

3. (5,5)

4. (0,-2)

5. (2,3)

6. (-4,-3)

7. (-3,2)

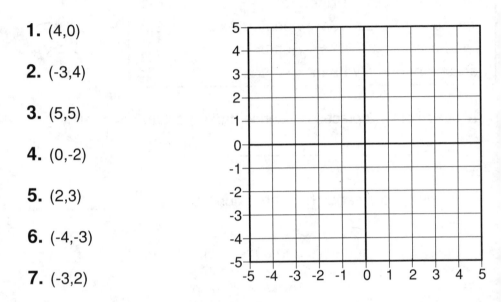

Use the coordinate system below to fill in the missing points.

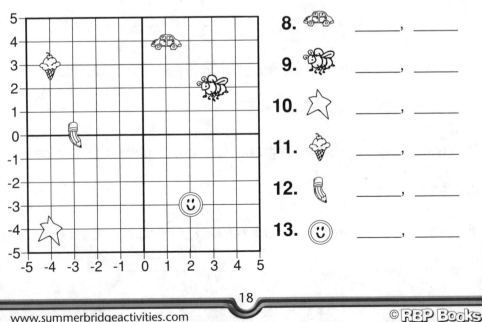

8. _____ , _____

9. _____ , _____

10. _____ , _____

11. _____ , _____

12. _____ , _____

13. _____ , _____

© RBP Books

Use the coordinate system below to fill in the missing points.

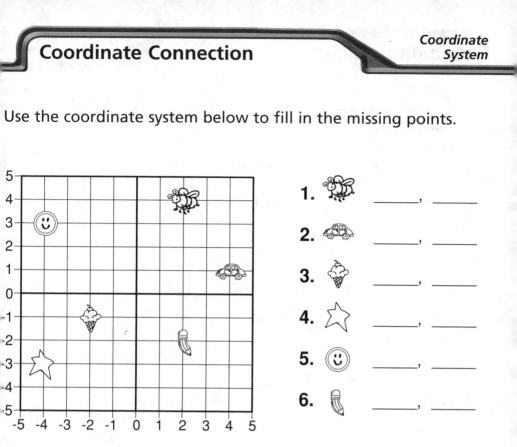

1. _____ , _____

2. _____ , _____

3. _____ , _____

4. _____ , _____

5. _____ , _____

6. _____ , _____

Plot the points on the coordinate system below.

7. (5,3)

8. (-4,2)

9. (1,4)

10. (0,-3)

11. (2,1)

12. (-4,-4)

13. (4,-1)

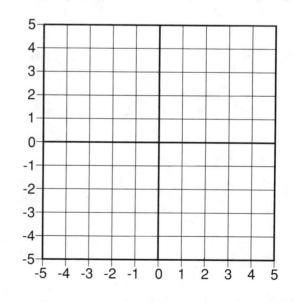

©RBP Books

Math Grade 4—RBP0032

Geometry Gems

REMEMBER...

Parallel lines never meet.
Perpendicular lines form a right angle where they meet.

Draw a red line parallel to each line segment below.

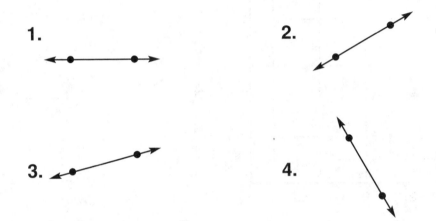

1.

2.

3.

4.

Draw a blue line perpendicular to each line segment below.

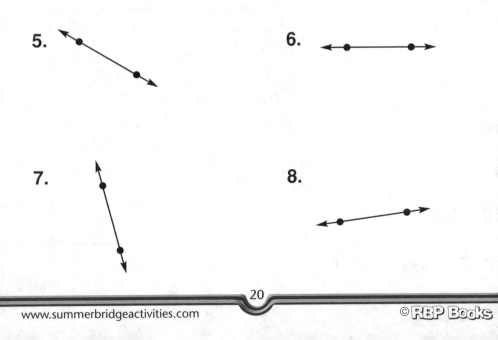

5.

6.

7.

8.

©RBP Books

Draw a line to match each shape with its correct name.

trapezoid

parallelogram

triangle

square

rectangle

pentagon

circle

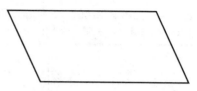

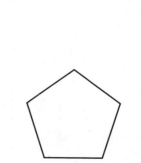

©RBP Books

Math Grade 4—RBP0032

Find the perimeter of each shape below.

> ## Remember...
> The **perimeter** is the distance around a figure. To find the perimeter of a figure, add up the lengths of each side of the figure.

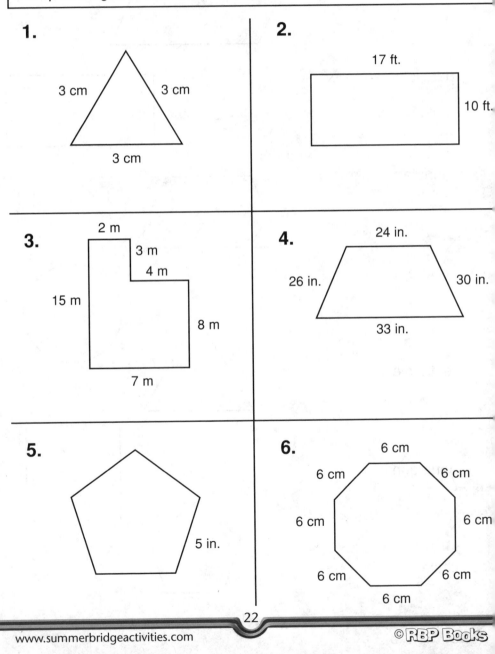

1.

3 cm   3 cm

3 cm

2.

17 ft.

10 ft.

3.

2 m
3 m
4 m
15 m
8 m
7 m

4.

24 in.

26 in.   30 in.

33 in.

5.

5 in.

6.

6 cm
6 cm   6 cm
6 cm   6 cm
6 cm   6 cm
6 cm

©RBP Books

Solve each problem. Draw a picture to help you figure the answer.

1. Maya is building a dog pen. Two of the sides are 24 feet, and the other two sides are 16 feet. How much fencing will Maya need?_____

2. Jackson is building a fence for his yard. His backyard measures 25 feet by 37 feet. How many feet of fencing will Jackson need to buy? _____

3. Hanna is putting a border of wallpaper along the top of her kitchen walls. Her kitchen measures 24 feet by 16 feet. How many feet of wallpaper will Hanna need to put up?

_____

4. Becca needs enough ribbon to go around the perimeter of her quilt. If the quilt measures 108 inches by 90 inches, how many inches of ribbon will Becca need to buy?

_____

5. Stan is making a frame for a picture he painted. The picture is 47 inches by 67 inches. How many inches around will his finished frame be? _____

6. Marie is making a flower garden in her yard. What is the perimeter of her garden if each edge measures 58 feet?

_____

©RBP Books

Find the area of each object.

REMEMBER...

To find the **area** of a rectangular figure, multiply the length by the width.

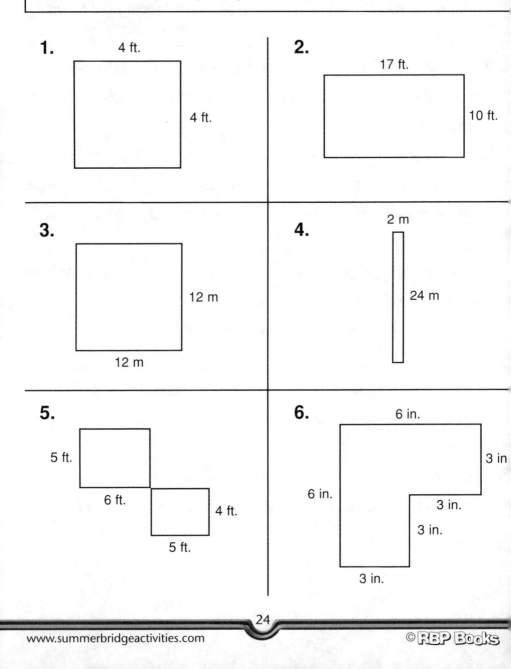

1.

4 ft.

4 ft.

2.

17 ft.

10 ft.

3.

12 m

12 m

4.

2 m

24 m

5.

5 ft.

6 ft.

4 ft.

5 ft.

6.

6 in.

3 in

6 in.

3 in.

3 in.

3 in.

©RBP Books

Ashley and her friends are working at the community center. Help them solve the problems. Remember to write the unit in your answer.

1. Ashley measures the area for the window. The window measures 14 inches wide and 32 inches tall. What is the area of the window? _____

2. Dylan wants to paint the back door to the center. The door is 58 inches tall and 28 inches wide. What is the area of the door?

_____

3. Matt and Haley are going to paint the floor in the gym. They need to figure out the area so they will know how much paint to buy. The floor is 132 inches by 347 inches. What is the area of the floor?

_____

4. Ashley wants to carpet a space that is 58 inches by 47 inches. What is the area of the space she wants to carpet?

_____

5. Rosa makes a small flower garden outside the center. The garden is 43 meters wide and 28 meters long. What is the area of Rosa's garden? _____

6. Dylan makes a table that is 77 inches wide and 49 inches long. What is the area of Dylan's table?

_____

©RBP Books

Work each problem. Write the letter from the box on the line below that matches the answer.

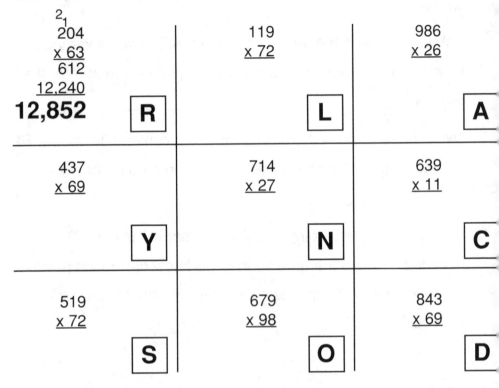

$$^2_1$$
204
x 63
612
12,240
12,852 R

119
x 72 L

986
x 26 A

437
x 69 Y

714
x 27 N

639
x 11 C

519
x 72 S

679
x 98 O

843
x 69 D

In 1903, Edwin Binney and C. Harold Smith made their first box of these.

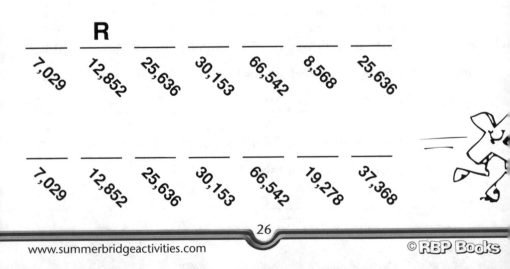

R

7,029 12,852 25,636 30,153 66,542 8,568 25,636

7,029 12,852 25,636 30,153 66,542 19,278 37,368

©RBP Books

Work each problem. Write the letter from the box on the line below that matches the answer.

543 x 42 **S**	453 x 64 **V**	963 x 66 **A**
511 x 52 **E**	124 x 73 **I**	896 x 43 **C**
7,432 x 2 **L**	5,327 x 5 **O**	7,621 x 7 **R**

In 2000, this was the most popular color of sports car sold.

_____ _____ _____ _____ _____ _____
22,806   9,052   14,864   28,992   26,572   53,347

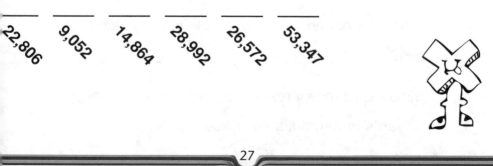

© RBP Books

Math Grade 4—RBP0032

Draw lines between equal measurements.

1.	24 inches	24 inches
2.	6 feet	27 feet
3.	9 yards	108 inches
4.	2 feet	2 feet
5.	48 inches	4 feet
6.	3 yards	2 yards

> 12 inches = 1 foot
> 3 feet = 1 yard

Solve each problem.

1. Sammy needs 108 inches of ribbon. How many yards does she need to buy? _____

2. Jason needs 12 feet of string for his project. How many yards should he buy? _____

3. Jennifer buys 8 yards of fabric. How many feet of fabric does she have? _____

4. Shawn is 6 feet and 7 inches tall. How many inches tall is Shawn? _____

5. Jasmine's quilt measures 396 inches around the edge. How many yards of trim does she need to buy? _____

Draw lines between equal measurements.

1. 8 quarts   5 tablespoons

2. 6 cups   4 pounds

3. 64 ounces   2 gallons

4. 12 pints   12 tablespoons

5. 36 teaspoons   6 quarts

6. 15 teaspoons   3 pints

1 tablespoon = 3 teaspoons
1 pint = 2 cups
1 quart = 2 pints
1 gallon = 4 quarts
1 pound = 16 ounces

Solve each problem.

1. Jessica is making cookies. She uses 64 ounces of chocolate chips in her recipe. How many pounds of chocolate chips does she need to have? _____

2. Maria's pie recipe calls for 10 pints of chopped fruit. How many quarts of chopped fruit does she need?

   _____

3. Larry needs 20 quarts of hot chocolate for the party. How many gallons should he buy? _____

4. Jack bottles 3 gallons of root beer. He sells his root beer in quart bottles. How many bottles does he need?

   _____

©RBP Books

It's a Fact!

Write the missing answer.

1. $9 \times 9 = \underline{\hspace{1cm}}$ **2.** $11\overline{)66} = \underline{\hspace{1cm}}$ **3.** $4 = \underline{\hspace{1cm}}\overline{)12}$

4. $7 = 6\overline{)\underline{\hspace{1cm}}}$ **5.** $9 = \underline{\hspace{1cm}}\overline{)81}$ **6.** $8 = 6\overline{)\underline{\hspace{1cm}}}$

7. $\underline{\hspace{1cm}} = 6\overline{)36}$ **8.** $\underline{\hspace{1cm}} = 12\overline{)144}$ **9.** $4 = \underline{\hspace{1cm}}\overline{)28}$

10. $\underline{\hspace{1cm}} = 4\overline{)32}$ **11.** $20 = \underline{\hspace{1cm}} \times 4$ **12.** $6 \times \underline{\hspace{1cm}} = 36$

13. $\underline{\hspace{1cm}} = 11\overline{)88}$ **14.** $54 = \underline{\hspace{1cm}} \times 9$ **15.** $9 \times \underline{\hspace{1cm}} = 72$

Missing
numerals?
I'm on the case!

©RBP Books

Work each problem. Draw a line to match the problem with the correct answer.

1.
$$\begin{array}{r} 45 \\ \times\,6 \\ \hline \end{array}$$
228

2.
$$\begin{array}{r} 19 \\ \times\,9 \\ \hline \end{array}$$
882

3.
$$\begin{array}{r} 76 \\ \times\,3 \\ \hline \end{array}$$
420

4.
$$\begin{array}{r} 58 \\ \times\,7 \\ \hline \end{array}$$
329

5.
$$\begin{array}{r} 98 \\ \times\,9 \\ \hline \end{array}$$
270

6.
$$\begin{array}{r} 84 \\ \times\,5 \\ \hline \end{array}$$
162

7.
$$\begin{array}{r} 27 \\ \times\,6 \\ \hline \end{array}$$
406

8.
$$\begin{array}{r} 47 \\ \times\,7 \\ \hline \end{array}$$
171

© RBP Books

Work each problem.

1.

$$\begin{array}{r} 1 \\ 57 \\ \times\,21 \\ \hline 57 \\ +\,1{,}140 \\ \hline \mathbf{1{,}197} \end{array}$$

$$\begin{array}{r} 98 \\ \times\,47 \\ \hline \end{array}$$

$$\begin{array}{r} 65 \\ \times\,76 \\ \hline \end{array}$$

$$\begin{array}{r} 87 \\ \times\,40 \\ \hline \end{array}$$

2.

$$\begin{array}{r} 19 \\ \times\,32 \\ \hline \end{array}$$

$$\begin{array}{r} 92 \\ \times\,78 \\ \hline \end{array}$$

$$\begin{array}{r} 13 \\ \times\,12 \\ \hline \end{array}$$

$$\begin{array}{r} 88 \\ \times\,32 \\ \hline \end{array}$$

3.

$$\begin{array}{r} 45 \\ \times\,28 \\ \hline \end{array}$$

$$\begin{array}{r} 96 \\ \times\,54 \\ \hline \end{array}$$

$$\begin{array}{r} 37 \\ \times\,49 \\ \hline \end{array}$$

$$\begin{array}{r} 74 \\ \times\,87 \\ \hline \end{array}$$

4.

$$\begin{array}{r} 94 \\ \times\,41 \\ \hline \end{array}$$

$$\begin{array}{r} 58 \\ \times\,67 \\ \hline \end{array}$$

$$\begin{array}{r} 76 \\ \times\,25 \\ \hline \end{array}$$

$$\begin{array}{r} 21 \\ \times\,11 \\ \hline \end{array}$$

©RBP Books

Work each problem, and find the quotient.

1.
$$\begin{array}{r} \textbf{63} \\ 7\,)\overline{441} \\ \underline{-42} \\ 21 \\ \underline{-21} \end{array}$$

2. $2\,)\overline{28}$

3. $9\,)\overline{585}$

4. $8\,)\overline{216}$

5. $5\,)\overline{235}$

6. $4\,)\overline{76}$

7. $3\,)\overline{276}$

8. $4\,)\overline{108}$

9. $8\,)\overline{728}$

10. $6\,)\overline{522}$

11. $9\,)\overline{738}$

12. $4\,)\overline{312}$

13. $8\,)\overline{656}$

14. $7\,)\overline{483}$

15. $6\,)\overline{336}$

© RBP Books

Find the quotient.

1. $3\overline{)29}$ **9**r2
$\underline{-\ 27}$
  2

2. $4\overline{)34}$

3. $2\overline{)15}$

4. $6\overline{)43}$

5. $8\overline{)54}$

6. $3\overline{)67}$

7. $7\overline{)50}$

8. $5\overline{)67}$

9. $4\overline{)86}$

10. $4\overline{)54}$

11. $7\overline{)85}$

12. $2\overline{)25}$

13. $5\overline{)59}$

14. $2\overline{)35}$

15. $5\overline{)86}$

www.summerbridgeactivities.com ©RBP Books

Work each problem.

1. $\overset{\textbf{3}\text{r}25}{63\overline{)214}}$
$\underline{-189}$
25

2. $54\overline{)912}$

3. $84\overline{)946}$

4. $12\overline{)168}$

5. $37\overline{)857}$

6. $72\overline{)216}$

7. $11\overline{)131}$

8. $35\overline{)385}$

9. $41\overline{)214}$

10. $27\overline{)351}$

11. $92\overline{)368}$

12. $15\overline{)405}$

© RBP Books

Work each problem.

1. $43\overline{)346}$ **2.** $12\overline{)743}$

3. $64\overline{)743}$ **4.** $84\overline{)321}$

5. $10\overline{)907}$ **6.** $23\overline{)632}$

7. $11\overline{)854}$ **8.** $64\overline{)753}$

9. $15\overline{)364}$ **10.** $72\overline{)842}$

11. $88\overline{)578}$ **12.** $46\overline{)347}$

www.summerbridgeactivities.com   ©RBP Books

Favorite Amusement Park Rides

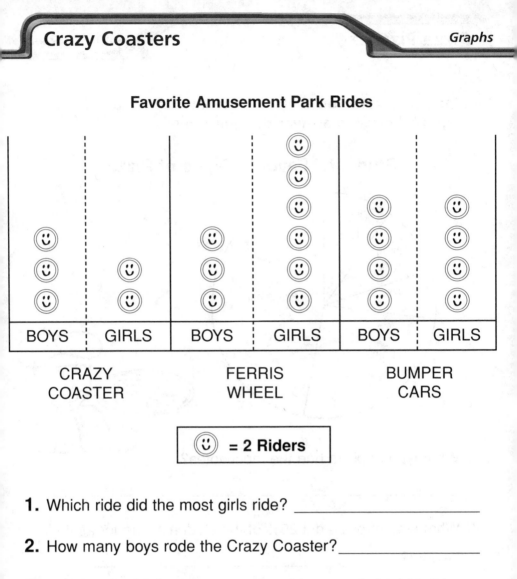

| BOYS | GIRLS | BOYS | GIRLS | BOYS | GIRLS |

CRAZY COASTER   FERRIS WHEEL   BUMPER CARS

☺ = 2 Riders

1. Which ride did the most girls ride? _____

2. How many boys rode the Crazy Coaster?_____

3. Which ride did the same number of boys and girls ride?

_____

4. How many boys rode on the Ferris wheel? _____

37

© RBP Books

Jasmine's class voted on their favorite kind of pizza. Use the circle graph below to answer the questions.

Students' Favorite Types of Pizza

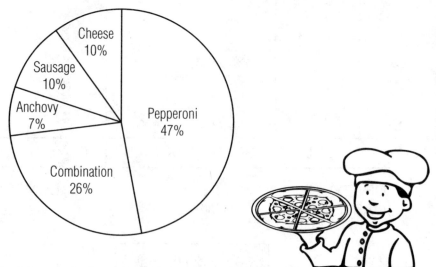

1. What type of pizza had the most votes?

_____

2. What type of pizza did 26% of the students vote for as their favorite? _____

3. What percentage of students voted for anchovy pizza as their favorite kind? _____

4. What was the percentage of students that liked combination and pepperoni pizza altogether? _____

5. Which two types of pizza had the same number of votes?

_____

www.summerbridgeactivities.com   ©RBP Books

Decimal Detectives

Write the missing numbers for the decimal values in the chart below.

	tenths	hundredths	thousandths
six-hundredths	**0**	**6**	
three-tenths			
twenty-five thousandths			
five-hundredths			
forty-seven thousandths			
seventy-two hundredths			
eight-thousandths			
ninety-nine hundredths			
sixty-seven thousandths			
one-tenth			

© RBP Books

Write the decimal number for each problem.

1. 1 and 9 tenths_____ **2.** 6 and 4 hundredths _____

3. 4 and 5 tenths_____ **4.** 7 and 33 thousandths _____

5. 2 and 6 hundredths _____ **6.** 9 and 14 hundredths _____

7. 5 and 8 tenths_____ **8.** 4 and 1 tenth _____

Write the decimal number.

1. $33\frac{5}{10}=$ _____ **2.** $71\frac{15}{100} =$ ____ **3.** $82\frac{16}{100} =$ _____

4. $604\frac{2}{100}=$ _____ **5.** $45\frac{6}{10} =$ ____ **6.** $401\frac{3}{10} =$ _____

7. $21\frac{27}{1000}=$ _____ **8.** $64\frac{7}{10} =$ ____ **9.** $906\frac{7}{10} =$ _____

10. $14\frac{9}{10}=$ _____ **11.** $99\frac{9}{1000} =$ ____ **12.** $23\frac{15}{100} =$ _____

©RBP Books

Digging for Decimals

Work each problem. Write the letter from the box on the line below that matches the answer.

1 1 1 24.98 +16.97 **41.95** **R**	421.00 − 34.79 **L**	64.39 + 7.21 **S**
97.06 − 9.72 **S**	649.07 + 21.99 **F**	84.72 + 16.99 **I**
64.9 − 5.7 **O**	90.54 + 45.58 **A**	643.79 − 98.47 **S**

What the paleontologist was digging for:

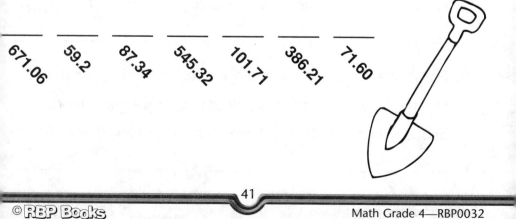

___ ___ ___ ___ ___ ___ ___
671.06 59.2 87.34 545.32 101.71 386.21 71.60

©RBP Books

Math Grade 4—RBP0032

Work each problem.

1. 22.91 – 7.27 = _____

2. 541.00 – 23.96 = _____

3. 4.4 + 72.1 + 2.89 = _____

4. 32.5 + 78.56 + 630.51 = _____

5. 88.45 – 54.1 = _____

6. 548.07 – 22.49 = _____

> ### Remember...
> To add and subtract decimals, you first line up the decimal points. Put in zeros for any missing numbers. Add or subtract. Remember to put the decimal point in the answer.

Solve each problem.

7. Jenny is measuring fossils. Fossil A measures 43.32 meters. Fossil B measures 32.98 meters. How much longer is Fossil A?

_____

8. Max is digging for a fossil. On the first day he digs 12.5 inches. The second day he digs 14.9 inches. The last day he digs 25.7 inches. How many inches did Max dig altogether? _____

_____

9. Samantha finds 2 rocks. The silver rock weighs 45.77 pounds, and the blue rock weighs 39.89 pounds. How many more pounds does the silver rock weigh than the blue rock? _____

_____

www.summerbridgeactivities.com   ©RBP Books

Marcy's class voted on their favorite food for lunch. Use the circle graph to answer the questions.

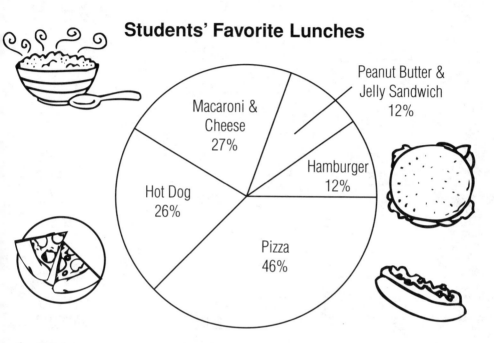

Students' Favorite Lunches

Peanut Butter & Jelly Sandwich 12%

Macaroni & Cheese 27%

Hamburger 12%

Hot Dog 26%

Pizza 46%

1. Which lunch received the highest number of votes?

_____

2. What percent of students voted for macaroni and cheese? _____

3. Which lunch did 46% of the students vote for as their favorite?

_____

4. What was the total percentage of students that liked pizza and hot dogs? _____

5. What percent fewer students voted for a peanut butter and jelly sandwich than a hot dog? _____

©RBP Books

Math Grade 4—RBP0032

Work each problem.

1.	52.07 − 9.19	2.	421.67 + 93.84	3.	5.51 + 6.70

4.	4.94 − 2.75	5.	6.4 5.9 + 2.3	6.	9.60 4.97 + 2.57

7.	35.21 − 9.87	8.	94.7 − 6.0	9.	11.97 + 6.98

Solve each problem.

10. Mario spent $2.91 on ice cream, $4.15 on plastic cups, and $15.87 on a cake. How much did Mario spend altogether? _____

11. Jan paid for her party supplies with a $20.00 bill. If the cost of her supplies was $18.48, how much change did she get back?

www.summerbridgeactivities.com

©RBP Books

Use the price list below to solve each problem.

Party Hats $6.43	Punch $9.93
Package of Candy $5.29	Paper Plates $3.86
Cake $13.67	Napkins $1.76
Ice Cream $2.56	Party Favors $7.98

1. Eric's mom wants him to buy ice cream, paper plates, and party hats. How much money does he need?

_____

2. Kendra buys 1 package of paper plates. She pays for the plates with a $10.00 bill. How much change will Kendra get back?

_____

3. Denzel buys one package of candy and a cake. How much does Denzel spend altogether? _____

4. Kim has $15.25. She buys 2 packages of napkins and punch. How much money does she have left? _____

5. Marc buys 1 package of party favors and 2 packages of napkins. His little sister wants a package of candy. Marc only has $18.00 in his wallet. Does he have enough money to buy the candy? _____

6. How much more does it cost to buy 1 package of party favors than to buy 1 package of party hats? _____

© RBP Books Math Grade 4—RBP0032

Zoe works at the Lots-of-Bargains car lot. The graph below shows how many cars Zoe has sold in the last six months.

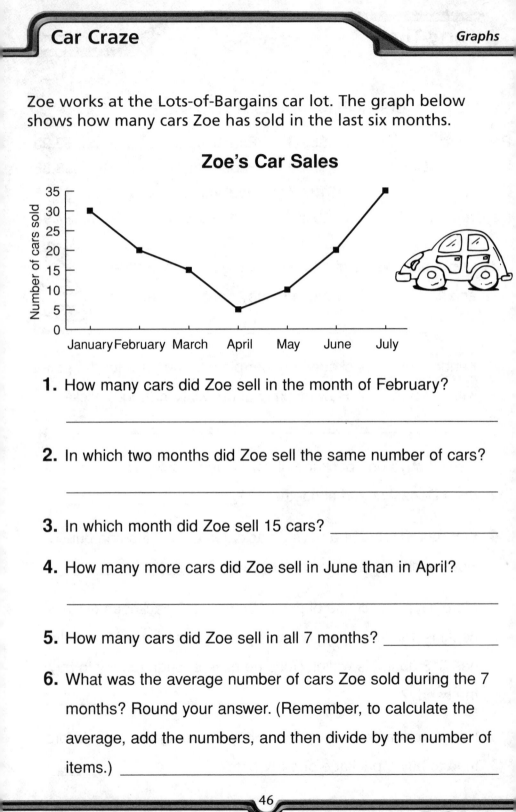

Zoe's Car Sales

1. How many cars did Zoe sell in the month of February?

_____

2. In which two months did Zoe sell the same number of cars?

_____

3. In which month did Zoe sell 15 cars? _____

4. How many more cars did Zoe sell in June than in April?

_____

5. How many cars did Zoe sell in all 7 months? _____

6. What was the average number of cars Zoe sold during the 7 months? Round your answer. (Remember, to calculate the average, add the numbers, and then divide by the number of items.) _____

©RBP Books

Use the graph to answer the questions.

Admit One
to the Movies!

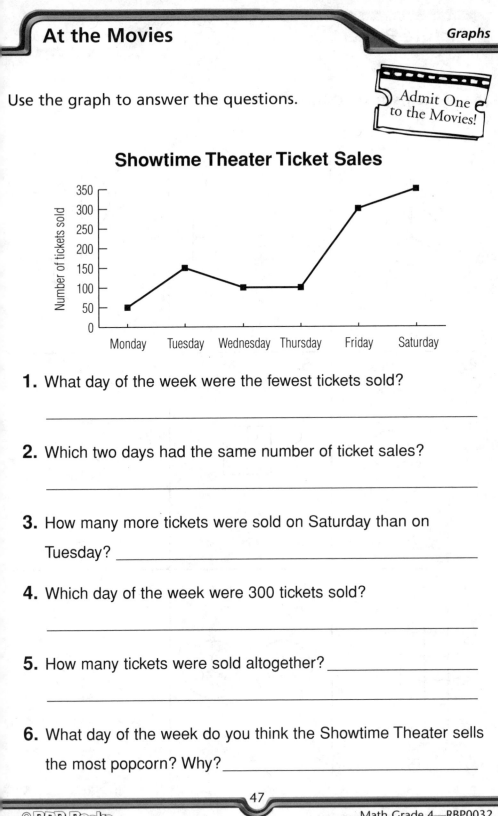

Showtime Theater Ticket Sales

1. What day of the week were the fewest tickets sold?

_____

2. Which two days had the same number of ticket sales?

_____

3. How many more tickets were sold on Saturday than on

Tuesday? _____

4. Which day of the week were 300 tickets sold?

_____

5. How many tickets were sold altogether? _____

_____

6. What day of the week do you think the Showtime Theater sells

the most popcorn? Why?_____

47

© RBP Books

Shade the parts that show the fraction.

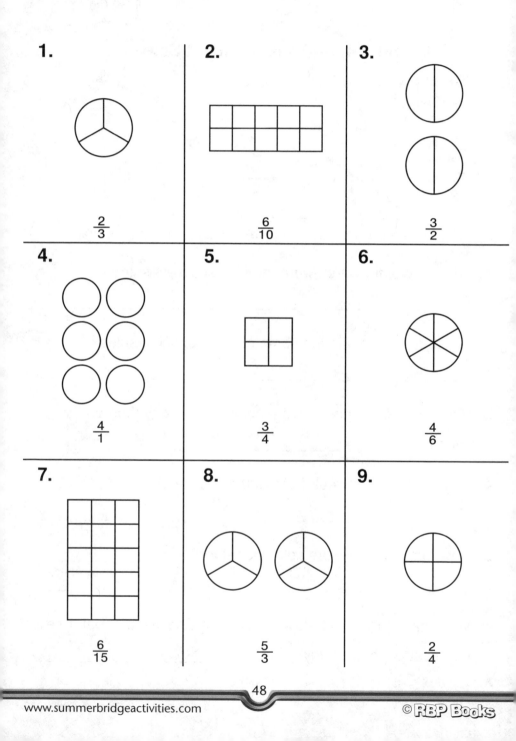

1.

$\frac{2}{3}$

2.

$\frac{6}{10}$

3.

$\frac{3}{2}$

4.

$\frac{4}{1}$

5.

$\frac{3}{4}$

6.

$\frac{4}{6}$

7.

$\frac{6}{15}$

8.

$\frac{5}{3}$

9.

$\frac{2}{4}$

© RBP Books

Picture Perfect

Write the fraction for each picture.

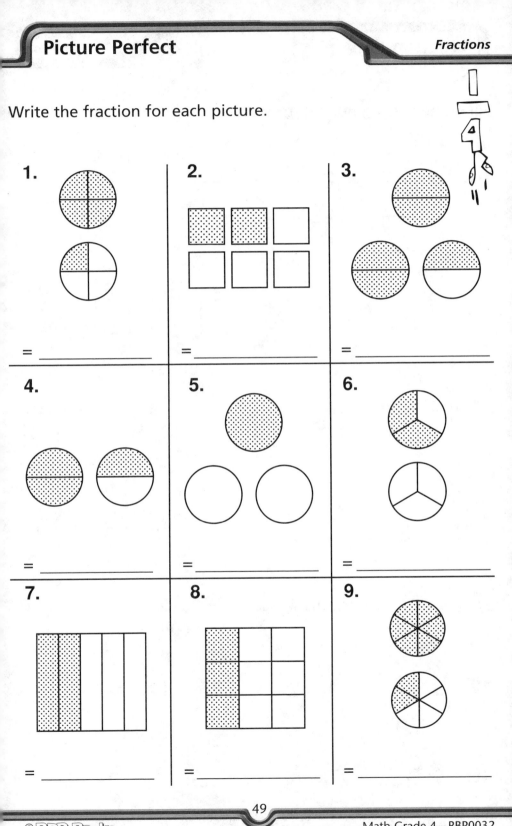

1.

= _____

2.

= _____

3.

= _____

4.

= _____

5.

= _____

6.

= _____

7.

= _____

8.

= _____

9.

= _____

© RBP Books

Fill in the missing number to complete the equivalent fraction.

1. $\frac{1}{4} = \frac{4}{\boxed{}}$

2. $\frac{2}{3} = \frac{8}{\boxed{}}$

3. $\frac{\boxed{}}{2} = \frac{7}{14}$

4. $\frac{3}{8} = \frac{\boxed{}}{24}$

5. $\frac{7}{8} = \frac{49}{\boxed{}}$

6. $\frac{10}{\boxed{}} = \frac{5}{8}$

7. $\frac{1}{\boxed{}} = \frac{4}{36}$

8. $\frac{3}{\boxed{}} = \frac{21}{28}$

9. $\frac{18}{45} = \frac{2}{\boxed{}}$

10. $\frac{2}{1} = \frac{24}{\boxed{}}$

11. $\frac{9}{12} = \frac{3}{\boxed{}}$

12. $\frac{2}{\boxed{}} = \frac{14}{63}$

Write each fraction in the lowest terms.

13. $\frac{4}{8} = $ _____

14. $\frac{9}{27} = $ _____

15. $\frac{8}{64} = $ _____

16. $\frac{24}{48} = $ _____

17. $\frac{15}{20} = $ _____

18. $\frac{27}{45} = $ _____

www.summerbridgeactivities.com   © RBP Books

Fraction Fun

Circle the equivalent fractions.

1. $\frac{1}{2}$ = $\boxed{\frac{2}{4}}$ $\frac{3}{4}$ $\frac{4}{16}$ $\frac{4}{6}$ $\boxed{\frac{10}{20}}$

2. $\frac{3}{8}$ = $\frac{1}{8}$ $\frac{3}{16}$ $\frac{6}{16}$ $\frac{12}{32}$ $\frac{16}{32}$

3. $\frac{1}{4}$ = $\frac{2}{4}$ $\frac{2}{5}$ $\frac{6}{12}$ $\frac{2}{8}$ $\frac{3}{12}$

4. $\frac{2}{3}$ = $\frac{2}{6}$ $\frac{4}{6}$ $\frac{4}{12}$ $\frac{6}{9}$ $\frac{10}{15}$

5. $\frac{2}{5}$ = $\frac{4}{10}$ $\frac{4}{14}$ $\frac{4}{5}$ $\frac{6}{15}$ $\frac{8}{20}$

6. $\frac{1}{7}$ = $\frac{2}{7}$ $\frac{7}{14}$ $\frac{2}{14}$ $\frac{3}{14}$ $\frac{3}{21}$

7. $\frac{3}{10}$ = $\frac{6}{10}$ $\frac{7}{10}$ $\frac{3}{30}$ $\frac{9}{30}$ $\frac{9}{10}$

8. $\frac{4}{5}$ = $\frac{8}{10}$ $\frac{8}{15}$ $\frac{12}{15}$ $\frac{4}{16}$ $\frac{12}{16}$

Fill in the missing number.

9. $\frac{1}{4} = \frac{3}{\boxed{}}$

10. $\frac{2}{\boxed{}} = \frac{4}{6}$

11. $\frac{5}{8} = \frac{\boxed{}}{16}$

12. $\frac{3}{4} = \frac{9}{\boxed{}}$

13. $\frac{\boxed{}}{6} = \frac{2}{12}$

14. $\frac{2}{3} = \frac{\boxed{}}{9}$

© RBP Books

Cookie Cut-ups

Rewrite each fraction as a mixed number.

1. $\frac{14}{3}$ = $4\frac{2}{3}$ 2. $\frac{16}{5}$ = _____   3. $\frac{13}{5}$ = _____

4. $\frac{9}{8}$ = _____   5. $\frac{13}{8}$ = _____   6. $\frac{21}{6}$ = _____

7. $\frac{19}{3}$ = _____   8. $\frac{7}{5}$ = _____   9. $\frac{10}{4}$ = _____

10. $\frac{11}{5}$ = _____   11. $\frac{8}{7}$ = _____   12. $\frac{14}{6}$ = _____

13. $\frac{15}{7}$ = _____   14. $\frac{19}{17}$ = _____   15. $\frac{12}{5}$ = _____

Solve each problem. Rewrite your answer as a mixed number.

16. Liz is tripling her cookie recipe. If her recipe calls for 3/4 cups of chocolate chips, how many cups of chocolate chops will she need altogether. _____

_____

17. Dexter's recipe calls for 5/8 tablespoon of baking soda. If he doubles his recipe, how many tablespoons of soda will he use altogether? _____

_____

©RBP Books

Cookie Cut-ups

Lucy is making cookies for her school's carnival. She is tripling her recipe. Help her triple the fractions in her recipe and change them to mixed numbers.

oatmeal	$\frac{9}{4}$ cups	**6 $\frac{3}{4}$ cups**
flour	$\frac{14}{3}$ cups	
sugar	$1\frac{1}{3}$ cups	
chocolate chips	$\frac{7}{2}$ cups	
butter	$\frac{5}{4}$ cups	
vanilla	$\frac{9}{8}$ tablespoons	

Rewrite the fraction as a mixed number.

1. $\frac{68}{11}$ = _____

2. $\frac{26}{5}$ = _____

3. $\frac{30}{4}$ = _____

4. $\frac{3}{2}$ = _____

5. $\frac{75}{9}$ = _____

6. $\frac{39}{6}$ = _____

7. $\frac{81}{8}$ = _____

8. $\frac{67}{8}$ = _____

9. $\frac{11}{4}$ = _____

10. $\frac{91}{10}$ = _____

11. $\frac{59}{7}$ = _____

12. $\frac{17}{7}$ = _____

© RBP Books

Fraction, Decimal, or Percent

Write the missing fraction, decimal, or percent in the chart below.

Fraction	Decimal	Percent
$\frac{2}{100}$	.02	2%
$\frac{51}{100}$		
	.45	
		19%
	.15	
		30%
$\frac{46}{100}$		
		27%
	.08	
$\frac{92}{100}$		
	.87	
		63%
$\frac{5}{100}$		

©RBP Books

Fraction, Decimal, or Percent

Write the decimal for each fraction.

1. $\frac{6}{100}$ = _____ 2. $\frac{25}{1000}$ = _____ 3. $\frac{3}{10}$ = _____

4. $\frac{8}{1000}$ = _____ 5. $\frac{2}{100}$ = _____ 6. $\frac{45}{100}$ = _____

7. $\frac{68}{100}$ = _____ 8. $\frac{1}{1000}$ = _____ 9. $\frac{4}{10}$ = _____

Write the fraction for each decimal.

1. .5 = _____ 2. .098 = _____ 3. .25 = _____

4. .004 = _____ 5. .7 = _____ 6. .76 = _____

7. .034 = _____ 8. .54 = _____ 9. .008 = _____

Write the percent for each decimal.

1. .05 = _____ 2. .80 = _____ 3. .10 = _____

4. .064 = _____ 5. .417 = _____ 6. .76 = _____

7. .244 = _____ 8. .54 = _____ 9. .101 = _____

© RBP Books   Math Grade 4—RBP0032

Write the fraction that goes with each picture.

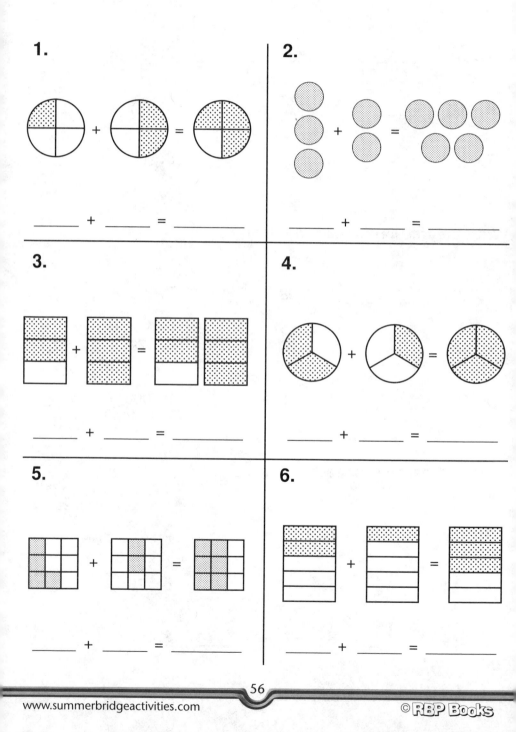

1.

_____ + _____ = _____

2.

_____ + _____ = _____

3.

_____ + _____ = _____

4.

_____ + _____ = _____

5.

_____ + _____ = _____

6.

_____ + _____ = _____

www.summerbridgeactivities.com   ©RBP Books

Work each problem.

1. $\frac{2}{4}$
    $+ \frac{1}{4}$
    $\overline{\ \frac{\mathbf{3}}{\mathbf{4}}\ }$

2. $\frac{4}{8}$
    $+ \frac{3}{8}$

3. $\frac{7}{16}$
    $- \frac{2}{16}$

4. $\frac{3}{4}$
    $- \frac{1}{4}$

5. $\frac{12}{12}$
    $- \frac{7}{12}$

6. $\frac{1}{6}$
    $+ \frac{4}{6}$

7. $\frac{7}{3}$
    $- \frac{6}{3}$

8. $\frac{2}{5}$
    $+ \frac{1}{5}$

9. $\frac{4}{15}$
    $+ \frac{7}{15}$

10. $\frac{25}{16}$
     $- \frac{20}{16}$

11. $\frac{3}{19}$
     $+ \frac{4}{19}$

12. $\frac{7}{7}$
     $+ \frac{9}{7}$

13. $\frac{3}{8}$
     $\frac{5}{8}$
     $+ \frac{7}{8}$

14. $\frac{6}{14}$
     $\frac{3}{14}$
     $+ \frac{9}{14}$

15. $\frac{9}{12}$
     $\frac{12}{12}$
     $+ \frac{5}{12}$

© RBP Books

Add or subtract. Write your answers in simplest terms. Rewrite improper fractions as mixed numbers.

1.
$$\frac{6}{15}$$
$$+ \frac{9}{15}$$

2.
$$\frac{3}{4}$$
$$+ \frac{3}{4}$$

3.
$$\frac{6}{8}$$
$$- \frac{2}{8}$$

4.
$$\frac{12}{4}$$
$$- \frac{5}{4}$$

5.
$$\frac{20}{10}$$
$$- \frac{7}{10}$$

6.
$$\frac{11}{9}$$
$$+ \frac{4}{9}$$

7.
$$\frac{7}{3}$$
$$- \frac{2}{3}$$

8.
$$\frac{6}{12}$$
$$- \frac{2}{12}$$

9.
$$\frac{15}{8}$$
$$- \frac{7}{8}$$

10. $\frac{4}{5} + \frac{11}{5} =$ _____

11. $\frac{1}{3} + \frac{9}{3} =$ _____

12. $\frac{5}{6} + \frac{3}{6} =$ _____

13. $\frac{2}{9} + \frac{5}{9} =$ _____

14. $\frac{7}{10} + \frac{4}{10} =$ _____

15. $\frac{2}{3} + \frac{3}{3} =$ _____

©RBP Books

Bug Sightings

For Beth's science project, she tracked how many bugs she could find in her backyard for seven days. Here are the results she recorded.

Day of the Week:	Number of Bug Sightings:
Sunday	13
Monday	10
Tuesday	9
Wednesday	9
Thursday	7
Friday	5
Saturday	4

1. What is the range of the bug sightings? _____

2. What is the mode of the bug sightings? _____

3. What is the median of the bug sightings? _____

4. What is the average number of bugs Beth sighted? _____

Remember...
- The **range** is the difference between the highest number and the lowest number in the data.
- To calculate the **mean** (or average), add the list of numbers, and then divide by the number of items.
- The **median** is the middle number that appears in the data.
- The **mode** is the number that appears most often in the data.

© RBP Books

The Bulldogs kept track of their scores from their last 7 basketball games. Here are their scores:

97

92

88

83

83

75

69

1. What is the range of the basketball scores? _____

2. What is the mode of the basketball scores? _____

3. What is the median of the basketball scores?_____

4. What is the mean of the basketball scores? _____

©RBP Books

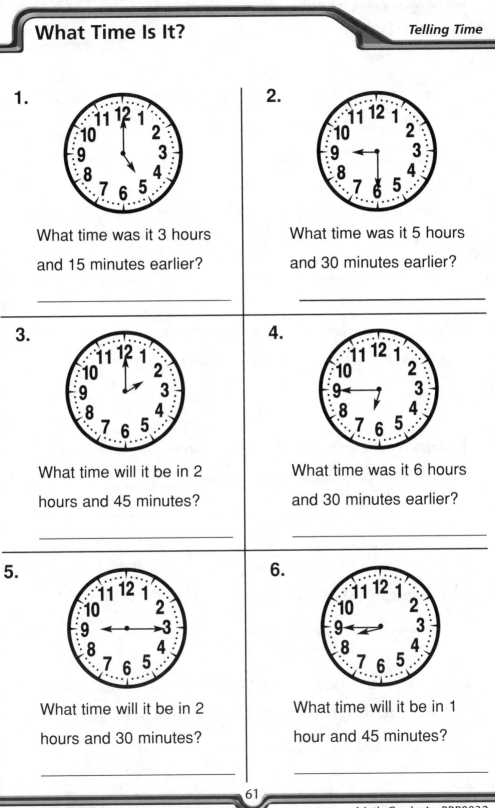

1.

What time was it 3 hours and 15 minutes earlier?

_____

2.

What time was it 5 hours and 30 minutes earlier?

_____

3.

What time will it be in 2 hours and 45 minutes?

_____

4.

What time was it 6 hours and 30 minutes earlier?

_____

5.

What time will it be in 2 hours and 30 minutes?

_____

6.

What time will it be in 1 hour and 45 minutes?

_____

© RBP Books   Math Grade 4—RBP0032

1. Max left for work at 7:30 a.m. He drove for 20 minutes. What time did he get to work? _____

_____

2. Lionel left 35 minutes before his swimming lesson. If his swimming lesson was at 9:45 a.m., what time did Lionel leave?

_____

3. Stacy has 45 minutes left before the library closes. It is 9:05 p.m. What time does the library close? _____

_____

4. Anne left the concert at 11:15 p.m. and drove home in 25 minutes. What time did Anne get home?_____

_____

5. Jackson was 25 minutes early for the party. If the party started at 6:45 p.m., what time did Jackson arrive at the party?

_____

6. Kara left her house at 7:45 a.m. She drove for 35 minutes and then stopped to buy a soda. What time did Kara stop?

_____

©RBP Books

Work each problem. Then put the answer in the puzzle below.

Across

1.   9,464
      + 6,756

4.   23
           457
         + 789

6.   32,167
       + 9,678

8.   9,787
        − 987

Down

2.   5,463
         x   4

3.   653
           x 56

4.   2,553
         − 743

5.   745
           − 78

7.   979
           + 129

Can
YOU
help solve
the puzzle?

© RBP Books

Work each problem. Then put the answer in the puzzle below.

Across

2.
$$\begin{array}{r} 2.5 \\ 89.8 \\ + \ 8.7 \\ \hline \end{array}$$

3.
$$\begin{array}{r} 53{,}785 \\ - \ 8{,}443 \\ \hline \end{array}$$

7.
$$\begin{array}{r} 6.553 \\ - \ 3.447 \\ \hline \end{array}$$

9.
$$\begin{array}{r} 56.787 \\ + \ 24.980 \\ \hline \end{array}$$

Down

1.
$$\begin{array}{r} 56{,}546 \\ \times \quad 9 \\ \hline \end{array}$$

4.
$$\begin{array}{r} 658 \\ \times \ \ 84 \\ \hline \end{array}$$

5.
$$\begin{array}{r} 896 \\ 567 \\ + \ 975 \\ \hline \end{array}$$

6.
$$\begin{array}{r} 6{,}753 \\ + \ 8{,}964 \\ \hline \end{array}$$

8.
$$\begin{array}{r} 123 \\ \times \ 53 \\ \hline \end{array}$$

© RBP Books

Weather Forecasting

Temperatures are measured in Fahrenheit and Celsius. Thirty-two degrees Fahrenheit is equal to zero degrees Celsius.

To convert a Fahrenheit temperature to Celsius:

Step 1: Subtract 32 from the Fahrenheit temperature value.

Step 2: Multiply by 5.

Step 3: Divide the result by 9.

Convert the temperatures to Celsius:

1. 41 degrees F _____

2. 68 degrees F _____

3. 95 degrees F _____

Convert the temperatures to Fahrenheit:

4. 50 degrees C _____

5. 25 degrees C _____

6. 45 degrees C _____

7. Which temperature is warmer, 41 degrees F or 50 degrees C?

_____

8. If water freezes at 32 degrees Fahrenheit, at what degree

Celsius will it freeze? _____

_____

© RBP Books

Weather Forecasting

Ann and Jamal observed the weather. They recorded the highest temperature and the lowest temperature each day for a week.

Day	High	Low
Sunday	87	42
Monday	88	42
Tuesday	87	41
Wednesday	85	40
Thursday	79	39
Friday	78	37
Saturday	73	36

1. What was the average high temperature for the week? _____

_____

2. What was the average low temperature for the week? _____

_____

3. Based on the temperatures Ann and Jamal recorded, what would you predict the temperatures for the next week will be? Why? _____

_____

4. Make a line graph in the space below to show the data.

©RBP Books

Dinner Dilemma

1. Mia is inviting her friends over for dinner. Her recipe makes enough for 13 people. If Mia has 39 friends coming, how many batches will she need to make?

_____

2. Help Mia convert her recipe so she will have enough servings for her friends.

Spaghetti Sauce:

1 can tomato sauce _____

2 pounds of tomatoes _____

$\frac{2}{3}$ cup chopped mushrooms _____

$\frac{1}{8}$ teaspoon salt _____

$\frac{1}{8}$ cup onion _____

$\frac{1}{4}$ teaspoon oregano _____

$\frac{3}{4}$ pound meat _____

3. If Mia doubles her original recipe, how many servings will she be short? _____

_____

4. What could she do so she would have enough food to serve every guest? _____

_____

© RBP Books

Dinner Dilemma

Shopping List	
Spaghetti $1.30	Mushrooms $1.59
Meat $3.57	Tomato sauce. . . $0.68
Bread. $1.47	Onions $1.29
Paper plates. . . . $3.71	Cookies $4.25

1. If Mia buys 1 of every item on her list, **estimate** how much it will cost. _____

2. Mia buys spaghetti, mushrooms, and tomato sauce. How much does she spend? _____

3. Mia buys cookies and paper plates. She pays with a $10.00 bill. How much change will Mia get back? _____

4. If Mia buys 3 cans of tomato sauce, 2 loaves of bread, and 1 package of spaghetti, how much will she spend altogether?

_____

5. Which costs more, 3 packages of meat or 2 packages of cookies? _____

6. If Mia has $15.00 in her wallet, how much change will she get back if she buys onions, meat, bread, and paper plates? _____

_____

7. How much more does 1 package of cookies cost than 1 package of meat? _____

©RBP Books

Map Making

Use the information to draw a map of Mario's neighborhood in the space below.

1. Key: 1/2 inch = 1 mile on the map.

2. The library is 8 miles east of Mario's house.

3. The gas station is 5 miles south of the library.

4. Zoe lives 4 miles from the library and 4 miles from Mario's house.

5. Jeff lives 8 miles west of the gas station.

6. The park is located between the library and Jeff's house.

7. The school is located 2.5 miles south of the library.

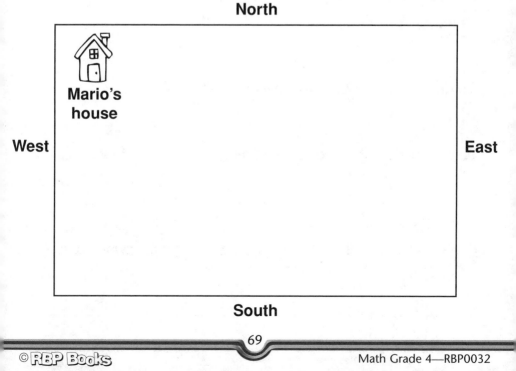

North

Mario's house

West

East

South

© RBP Books

Math Grade 4—RBP0032

Map Making

Use the map you made on the last page to answer the questions.

1. What is the distance between Mario's house and Zoe's house? _____

2. How many miles is it from Mario's house to the gas station?

   _____

3. How many miles is it from Jeff's house to the library?

   _____

4. If Mario goes to the library, to the gas station, to Jeff's house, and back home by the same route, how far does he travel?

   _____

5. How much farther is Jeff's house from Mario's than Zoe's house is from Mario's?

   _____

6. How far does Mario travel to school?

   _____

7. Who travels the shortest distance to school, Jeff, Zoe, or Mario?

   _____

8. Whose house is closest to the park? How far away do you think it is?

   _____

©RBP Books

Driving the Distance

Find the distance each driver went. Make a table to help you organize the information.

Brett drove 2,424 miles.

Eve drove half as many miles as Brett.

This is a great wake up exercise!

Sara drove 5 times as many miles as Eve.

Dean drove 1,487 miles less than Sara.

John drove 3 times as many miles as Dean.

Driver:	Mileage:
Brett	1.
Eve	2.
Sara	3.
Dean	4.
John	5.

© RBP Books

Math Grade 4—RBP0032

Driving the Distance

Work each problem. Use the information in the table from the last page.

1. Which driver had the most mileage?_____

2. How many more miles did John drive than Dean?

_____

3. If Eve's company reimburses her 23 cents for each mile she drives, how many dollars will she get?

_____

4. What was the average number of miles driven? Round your answer. _____

5. How many miles did Eve and Sara drive altogether?

_____

6. If Dean gets 16 miles per gallon of gas, how many gallons of gas did he use? _____

7. Brett drove 60 miles per hour. How many hours did he travel?

_____

8. Eve's car gets 17.8 miles per gallon of gas. Sara's car gets 23.1 miles per gallon of gas. How many more miles per gallon does Sara's car get than Eve's car?

_____

Answer Pages

Page 1

1. 30	40	40	70
2. 60	30	100	10
3. 80	60	50	80
4. 300	600	100	500
5. 900	500	500	700
6. 800	300	400	700
7. 8,000	5,000	4,000	4,000
8. 3,000	8,000	6,000	1,000
9. 2,000	2,000	5,000	1,000

Page 2

1. 21,500	2. 9,000	3. 214,000
4. 720	5. 6,000	6. 3,300
7. 611,600	8. 60	9. 20
10. 50	11. 1,400	12. 3,400
13. 200		

Page 3

Anchorage, Alaska	260,000	260,300
Sedona, Arizona	10,000	10,200
Oceanside, California	161,000	161,000
Boca Raton, Florida	75,000	74,800
Burley, Idaho	9,000	9,300
Sioux City, Iowa	85,000	85,000
Baton Rouge, Louisiana	228,000	227,800
Jackson, Missouri	12,000	11,900
Missoula, Montana	57,000	57,100
Las Vegas, Nevada	478,000	478,400
Aztec, New Mexico	6,000	6,400
Albany, New York	96,000	95,700
El Paso, Texas	564,000	563,700
Salt Lake City, Utah	182,000	181,700

Page 4

1. 9,221	2. 32,064	3. 849
4. 783,600	5. 495	6. 888,725

7. two thousand nine hundred forty-three
8. ten thousand eight hundred eleven
9. seven thousand two hundred forty-six
10. one hundred twelve thousand one hundred sixty-one
11. one thousand six hundred forty-one
12. ninety thousand twelve

Page 5

1. Fourteen, Maria Smith
2. 533.00, Maria Smith
3. Seven hundred eighty-four, Maria Smith

Page 6

1. 43,473	2. 55,627	3. 74,485
4. 458,147	5. 626,351	6. 850,528
7. 174,608	8. 1,210,420	

Page 7

1. 593	2. 14,650	3. 40,736
4. 154	5. 27,381	6. 3,464
7. 91,475	8. 763	

Page 8

1. 6,825	159,732	107,766	87,677
2. 94,214	104,935	88,111	101,183
3. 43,646	89,461	113,710	76,477
4. 20,001	22,279	17,564	20,750
5. 20,737	19,953	20,212	16,247

Page 9

1. 4,715	10,338	13,319	9,662
2. 85,344	175,497	84,918	73,149
3. 88,826	132,831	124,678	57,347
4. 486,674	1,589,732	1,328,167	721,014
5. 20,181	23,615	22,008	18,298

© RBP Books

Answer Pages

Page 10
1. >   2. <   3. >   4. >   5. >
6. =   7. >   8. <   9. >   10. =
11. <   12. <   13. >   14. >

Page 11
1. >   2. >   3. =   4. =   5. >
6. <   7. <   8. >   9. =   10. =
11. >   12. >

Page 12
1. 355	159	53	373
2. 94	99	595	245
3. 755	374	205	175
4. 594	1,156	124	1,434
5. 6,622	1,294	138	85

Page 13
1. 107	489	174	263
2. 477	688	118	569
3. 224	507	290	288
4. 2,225	4,154	3,096	1,134
5. 26,581	51,667	40,176	16,990

Page 15
1. $10.30   2. $.67   3. $17.04
4. no   5. $26.46   6. $4.56

Page 16
1. 50 + 90 + 70 = 210
2. 70 + 90 + 90 = 250
3. 60 + 100 + 40 = 200
4. 100 + 100 + 90 = 290
5. 40 + 60 + 80 = 180
6. 90 + 90 + 80 = 260
7. 70 + 70 + 80 = 220
8. 50 + 60 + 90 = 200

Page 17
1. $.80   2. $1.50   3. $1.30   4. $1.80
5. $1.60   6. $1.40   7. $1.80   8. $4.80

Page 18
(1–7)

8. (1,4)   9. (3,2)   10. (-4,-4)
11. (-4,3)   12. (-3,0)   13. (2,-3)

Page 19
1. (2,4)   2. (4,1)   3. (-2,-1)
4. (-4,-3)   5. (-4,3)   6. (2,-2)
(7–13)

Page 20
1.   2.

3.   4.

5.   6.

7.   8.

74

© RBP Books

Answer Pages

Page 21

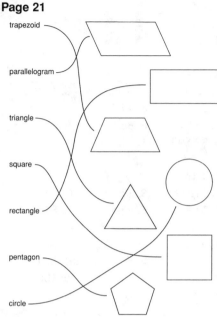

trapezoid

parallelogram

triangle

square

rectangle

pentagon

circle

Page 22
1. 9 centimeters   **2.** 54 feet
3. 39 meters   **4.** 113 inches
5. 25 inches   **6.** 48 centimeters

Page 23
1. 80 feet   **2.** 124 feet
3. 80 feet   **4.** 396 inches
5. 228 inches   **6.** 232 feet

Page 24
1. 16 sq. feet   **2.** 170 sq. feet
3. 144 sq. meters   **4.** 48 sq. meters
5. 50 sq. feet   **6.** 27 sq. inches

Page 25
1. 448 sq. inches   **2.** 1,624 sq. inches
3. 45,804 sq. inches   **4.** 2,726 sq. inches
5. 1,204 sq. meters   **6.** 3,773 sq. inches

Page 26
Crayola crayons

Page 27
silver

Page 28
1. 2 feet   **2.** 2 yards   **3.** 27 feet
4. 24 inches   **5.** 4 feet   **6.** 108 inches

1. 3 yards   **2.** 4 yards   **3.** 24 feet
4. 79 inches   **5.** 11 yards

Page 29
1. 2 gallons   **2.** 3 pints   **3.** 4 pounds
4. 6 quarts   **5.** 12 tablespoons
6. 5 tablespoons

1. 4 pounds   **2.** 5 quarts   **3.** 5 gallons
4. 12 quart bottles

Page 30
1. 81   **2.** 6   **3.** 3   **4.** 42   **5.** 9
6. 48   **7.** 6   **8.** 12   **9.** 7   **10.** 8
11. 5   **12.** 6   **13.** 8   **14.** 6   **15.** 8

Page 31
1. 270   **2.** 171   **3.** 228   **4.** 406
5. 882   **6.** 420   **7.** 162   **8.** 329

Page 32
1. 1,197   4,606   4,940   3,480
2. 608   7,176   156   2,816
3. 1,260   5,184   1,813   6,438
4. 3,854   3,886   1,900   231

Page 33
1. 63   **2.** 14   **3.** 65   **4.** 27   **5.** 47
6. 19   **7.** 92   **8.** 27   **9.** 91   **10.** 87
11. 82   **12.** 78   **13.** 82   **14.** 69   **15.** 56

Page 34
1. 9 r2   **2.** 8 r2   **3.** 7 r1   **4.** 7 r1
5. 6 r6   **6.** 22 r1   **7.** 7 r1   **8.** 13 r2
9. 21 r2   **10.** 13 r2   **11.** 12 r1   **12.** 12 r1
13. 11 r4   **14.** 17 r1   **15.** 17 r1

© RBP Books

Math Grade 4—RBP0032

Answer Pages

Page 35
1. 3 r25 2. 16 r48 3. 11 r22 4. 14
5. 23 r6 6. 3 7. 11 r10 8. 11
9. 5 r9 10. 13 11. 4 12. 27

Page 36
1. 8 r2 2. 61 r11 3. 11 r39 4. 3 r69
5. 90 r7 6. 27 r11 7. 77 r7 8. 11 r49
9. 24 r4 10. 11 r50 11. 6 r50 12. 7 r25

Page 37
1. Ferris wheel 2. 6 boys
3. bumper cars 4. 6 boys

Page 38
1. pepperoni 2. combination
3. 7% 4. 73%
5. cheese and sausage

Page 39
1. .06 2. .3 3. .025 4. .05
5. .047 6. .72 7. .008 8. .99
9. .067 10. .1

Page 40
1. 1.9 2. 6.04 3. 4.5 4. 7.033
5. 2.06 6. 9.14 7. 5.8 8. 4.1

1. 33.5 2. 71.15 3. 82.16 4. 604.02
5. 45.6 6. 401.3 7. 21.027 8. 64.7
9. 906.7 10. 14.9 11. 99.009 12. 23.15

Page 41
fossils

Page 42
1. 15.64 2. 517.04 3. 79.39
4. 741.57 5. 34.35 6. 525.58
7. 10.34 meters 8. 53.1 inches
9. 5.88 pounds

Page 43
1. pizza 2. 27% 3. pizza
4. 72% 5. 14%

Page 44
1. 42.88 2. 515.51 3. 12.21
4. 2.19 5. 14.6 6. 17.14
7. 25.34 8. 88.7 9. 18.95
10. $22.93 11. $1.52

Page 45
1. $12.85 2. $6.14 3. $18.96
4. $1.80 5. yes 6. $1.55

Page 46
1. 20 cars 2. February and June
3. March 4. 15 cars 5. 135 cars
6. 19 cars

Page 47
1. Monday
2. Wednesday and Thursday
3. 200 tickets
4. Friday
5. 1,050 tickets
6. Saturday, the day the most people come

Page 48

www.summerbridgeactivities.com

© RBP Books

Answer Pages

© RBP Books

Page 49
1. $\frac{5}{4}$ 2. $\frac{2}{6}$ 3. $\frac{5}{2}$
4. $\frac{3}{2}$ 5. $\frac{1}{1}$ 6. $\frac{2}{3}$
7. $\frac{2}{5}$ 8. $\frac{3}{9}$ 9. $\frac{8}{6}$

Page 50
1. 16   2. 12   3. 1   4. 9   5. 56
6. 16   7. 9   8. 4   9. 5   10. 12
11. 4   12. 9   13. $\frac{1}{2}$ 14. $\frac{1}{3}$ 15. $\frac{1}{8}$
16. $\frac{1}{2}$ 17. $\frac{3}{4}$ 18. $\frac{3}{5}$

Page 51
1. $\frac{2}{4}$, $\frac{10}{20}$ 2. $\frac{6}{16}$, $\frac{12}{32}$ 3. $\frac{2}{8}$, $\frac{3}{12}$ 4. $\frac{4}{6}$, $\frac{6}{9}$, $\frac{10}{15}$
5. $\frac{4}{10}$, $\frac{6}{15}$, $\frac{8}{20}$ 6. $\frac{2}{14}$, $\frac{3}{21}$ 7. $\frac{9}{30}$ 8. $\frac{8}{10}$, $\frac{12}{15}$
9. 12   10. 3   11. 10   12. 12
13. 1   14. 6

Page 52
1. $4\frac{2}{3}$ 2. $3\frac{1}{1}$ 3. $2\frac{3}{5}$
4. $1\frac{1}{8}$ 5. $1\frac{5}{8}$ 6. $3\frac{3}{6}$ or $3\frac{1}{2}$
7. $6\frac{1}{3}$ 8. $1\frac{2}{5}$ 9. $2\frac{2}{4}$ or $2\frac{1}{2}$
10. $2\frac{1}{5}$ 11. $1\frac{1}{7}$ 12. $2\frac{2}{6}$ or $2\frac{1}{3}$
13. $2\frac{1}{7}$ 14. $1\frac{2}{17}$ 15. $2\frac{2}{5}$
16. $2\frac{1}{4}$ cups   17. $1\frac{2}{8}$ or $1\frac{1}{4}$ tablespoons

Page 53
oatmeal: $6\frac{3}{4}$ cups
flour: 14 cups
sugar: 4 cups
chocolate chips: $10\frac{1}{2}$ cups
butter: $3\frac{3}{4}$ cups
vanilla: $3\frac{3}{8}$ tablespoons

1. $6\frac{2}{11}$ 2. $5\frac{1}{5}$ 3. $7\frac{2}{4}$ or $7\frac{1}{2}$
4. $1\frac{1}{2}$ 5. $8\frac{3}{9}$ or $8\frac{1}{3}$ 6. $6\frac{3}{6}$ or $6\frac{1}{2}$
7. $10\frac{1}{8}$ 8. $8\frac{3}{8}$ 9. $2\frac{3}{4}$
10. $9\frac{1}{10}$ 11. $8\frac{3}{7}$ 12. $2\frac{3}{7}$

Page 54
1. $\frac{2}{100}$ .02   2%
2. $\frac{51}{100}$ .51   51%
3. $\frac{45}{100}$ .45   45%
4. $\frac{19}{100}$ .19   19%
5. $\frac{15}{100}$ .15   15%
6. $\frac{30}{100}$ .30   30%
7. $\frac{46}{100}$ .46   46%
8. $\frac{27}{100}$ .27   27%
9. $\frac{8}{100}$ .08   8%
10. $\frac{92}{100}$ .92   92%
11. $\frac{87}{100}$ .87   87%
12. $\frac{63}{100}$ .63   63%
13. $\frac{5}{100}$ .05   5%

Page 55
1. .06   2. .025   3. .3
4. .008   5. .02   6. .45
7. .68   8. .001   9. .4

1. $\frac{5}{10}$ 2. $\frac{98}{1000}$ 3. $\frac{25}{100}$
4. $\frac{4}{1000}$ 5. $\frac{7}{10}$ 6. $\frac{76}{100}$
7. $\frac{34}{1000}$ 8. $\frac{54}{100}$ 9. $\frac{8}{1000}$

1. 5%   2. 80%   3. 10%
4. 6.4%   5. 41.7%   6. 76%
7. 24.4%   8. 54%   9. 10.1%

Page 56
1. $\frac{1}{4} + \frac{2}{4} = \frac{3}{4}$ 2. $\frac{3}{1} + \frac{2}{1} = \frac{5}{1}$
3. $\frac{2}{3} + \frac{3}{3} = \frac{5}{3}$ 4. $\frac{2}{3} + \frac{1}{3} = \frac{3}{3}$
5. $\frac{4}{9} + \frac{2}{9} = \frac{6}{9}$ 6. $\frac{2}{5} + \frac{1}{5} = \frac{3}{5}$

Page 57
1. $\frac{3}{4}$ 2. $\frac{7}{8}$ 3. $\frac{5}{16}$
4. $\frac{4}{4}$ or $\frac{1}{2}$ 5. $\frac{5}{12}$ 6. $\frac{5}{6}$
7. $\frac{1}{3}$ 8. $\frac{3}{5}$ 9. $\frac{11}{15}$
10. $\frac{5}{16}$ 11. $\frac{7}{19}$ 12. $\frac{16}{7}$ or $2\frac{2}{7}$
13. $\frac{15}{8}$ or $1\frac{7}{8}$ 14. $\frac{18}{14}$ or $1\frac{2}{7}$ 15. $\frac{26}{12}$ or $2\frac{1}{6}$

Math Grade 4—RBP0032

Answer Pages

Page 58
1. 1   2. $1\frac{1}{2}$ 3. $\frac{1}{2}$ 4. $1\frac{3}{4}$
5. $1\frac{3}{10}$ 6. $1\frac{2}{3}$ 7. $1\frac{2}{3}$ 8. $\frac{1}{3}$
9. 1   10. 3   11. $3\frac{1}{3}$ 12. $1\frac{1}{3}$
13. $\frac{7}{9}$ 14. $1\frac{1}{10}$ 15. $1\frac{2}{3}$

Page 59
1. 9   2. 9   3. 9   4. 8.14 bugs

Page 60
1. 28   2. 83   3. 83   4. 83.86

Page 61
1. 1:45   2. 4:00   3. 4:45   4. 12:15
5. 11:45   6. 10:30

Page 62
1. 7:50 a.m.   2. 9:10 a.m.   3. 9:50 p.m.
4. 11:40 p.m.   5. 6:20 p.m.   6. 8:20 a.m.

Page 63
Across:
1. 16,220   4. 1,269   6. 41,845   8. 8,800
Down:
2. 21,852   3. 36,568   4. 1,810   5. 667
7. 1,108

Page 64
Across:
2. 101   3. 45,342   7. 3.106   9. 81.767
Down:
1. 508,914   4. 55,272   5. 2,438
6. 15,717   8. 6,519

Page 65
1. 5 degrees C   2. 20 degrees C
3. 35 degrees C   4. 122 degrees F
5. 77 degrees F   6. 113 degrees F
7. 50 degrees C   8. 0 degrees C

Page 66
1. 82.43
2. 39.57
3. Dropping into the 60s

Page 67
1. 3 batches
2. 3 cans tomato sauce
   6 pounds tomatoes
   2 cups mushrooms
   $\frac{3}{8}$ teaspoon salt
   $\frac{3}{8}$ cup onion
   $\frac{3}{4}$ teaspoon oregano
   $2\frac{1}{4}$ pounds meat
3. 13 servings
4. Answers will vary.

Page 68
1. approximately $18.00
2. $3.57   3. $2.04
4. $6.28   5. 3 packages of meat
6. $4.96   7. $.68

Page 70
1. 4 miles   2. 13 miles   3. 13 miles
4. 42 miles   5. 1 mile   6. 10.5 miles
7. Zoe   8. Zoe's, 2.5 miles

Page 71
1. 2,424   2. 1,212
3. 6,060   4. 4,573
5. 3,719

Page 72
1. John   2. 9,146 miles
3. $278.76   4. 5,598 miles
5. 7,272 miles   6. 285.81 gallons
7. 40.4 hours   8. 5.3 miles per gallon

78

www.summerbridgeactivities.com   © RBP Books